MW00777367

Inuit Poems and Songs

Folk poetry from
East Greenland

Adventures in New Lands: Volume 8

Inuit

Poems and Songs

Folk Poetry from
East Greenland

Collected and with Introduction
by William Thalbitzer

Translated by Torben Hutchings

International Polar Institute Press

Distributed by University Press of New England
upne.com

Originally published as
Eskimoiske Digte,
Copenhagen, 1920

Adventures in New Lands: Volume 8

Funded in part by a grant from
DANISH ARTS FOUNDATION
Copenhagen, Denmark

First English edition

ISBN 978-0-9961938-2-5

International Polar Institute Press
Post Office Box 212
Hanover, New Hampshire 03755 USA

Contents

Introduction

These poems sprang from the heart of east Greenland, by the farthest northern border of the sea of mankind, on one of the most desolate and harsh coasts. They were found there as part of a living tradition among a small, recently discovered group of Inuit, that I had travelled to in order to study a new Greenlandic dialect.[1] I heard them here for the first time as they sounded from the lips of the people, and as they must have sounded through many generations. I understood that this was some of the old poetry of the Inuit people, and that these songs and poems deserved to be preserved for a greater humanity.

How strange it was to find such a rich wealth of poetry amidst these desolate fells, such spiritual fecundity so far off the beaten track! Here, below the receding glacial borders of the last ice age, an otherworldly tribe of Mongolian-Indian racial mix live and build: a sea-hunting people, an outlier, who until recently knew nothing of books or of paper, but sharpened their chalcedony arrows and went about their hunting in blissful ignorance of geography and all modern inventions, worshipping only the spirits and gods of their own land—their myths, legends and hopes for the future—only the inner traditions of their souls, their ancient heathen wisdom and dreams of happiness.

The tribe had once been bigger. The Eskimos once built across the entire length of Greenland's east coast, which with its curves has a length comparable of that from Copenhagen to the Nile delta.

The 500 natives, who populate this coast—which in contrast to the west coast is depopulated and empty—as the last signs of human life, swarm around an archipelago village a little bit south of the midpoint of the coast, where it falls off in an east-west direction. Here lie the two great fjords of Sermilik, "The Ice River" and Ammassalik, "The Capelin Fjord" (from ammassak "capelin or dwarf trout"), amazingly beautiful inland seas between towering mountain peaks, which seem to rise row-on-row from the sea to eventually vanish in disorderly flocks beneath Greenland's inland ice.

At the coast of this settlement there are many famous fells: Orttunuviaq, Aneen, Oonuttoq, Asinaleq and Qalerajiviæn, which the Europeans call Cape Dan. The native settlements lie spread out across the islands and the fjord, each with their own old Greenlandic name, which do not roll easily off our tongues.

These fjords are full of legends and have the depth of eternity. They shimmer with white ice that shoots in, torn from the sea's mile-wide flow, then slowly and steadily moves out at the outermost reefs.

The ice flow of the polar sea is ground by the earth's very own mill in unknown regions to the north; it perpetually drifts from north to south, along the length of the Greenlandic coast, an unending stream that stands out noticeably and mightily in the Atlantic ocean, almost like the milky way in the sky. Always it rubs itself along the coast in an irresistible slide towards the south, like a giant shining snake; one that spews forth its billowing fogs across the cliffs in the evening, then slowly wrap themselves around the granite edges and fill the valleys with their grey shivers. It is as if the settlement is swallowed by the sea, and the poor light of the blubber lanterns that shine through the gut-skin windows fades away in the impermeable gloom. It is then that the angakkok, the heathen priest, reaches for his magic drum in order to summon his spirits. The lust for life is wildly kindled in the small people therein, and the night resounds with the drumming songs of the dancing games. The overly grim seriousness of nature is met by the defiance of the sparks of laughter. It is not hard to drown out the fear of the dark when everyone is gathered between the walls of the hut.

These floating floes and flakes—they are pushed in from way out east—"the ices," as the natives say (*cikin*)—in through the straits of the archipelago, through the mouths of the fjords—

in the milk-blue water they bob up and down, twist, whirl, circle about in places where there is a current, gather around an ice-field like a pack of dogs around a polar bear—the ices shine and take on bluish hues in the crisp air, with the reflected light filling fjords and fells, and the eternal noise beats against the stone walls on both sides of the fjord; all the way into the hut— through the low rock-lined entrance passage— the distant rumble of the masses rubbing and breaking in the water penetrates a subdued and confusing mumbling with groans and sighs, a soft and oddly abrasive chatter—and now and again the mumbling rises into a muffled boom, when a floe cracks or when an ice-field calves. In the spring the sun's rays through the ice become twice as scintillating and alive, indeed quite crazy—these white, shining concentrations of light are gripped by an insane joy and leap about like mad between the snow-slick fells, between heaven and sea—the world has become akin to a kaleidoscope, with the light dancing and shining in from all sides— it attacks the eyes, people become snow blind, either that or they must ward off snow blindness by wearing heavy snow goggles—flat blocks which are cut out of a piece of driftwood with a small slit, through which the light gains a grudging entry: how odd the world looks through that slit!

Piece by piece and split into strands, the fjord ice and fells penetrate the darkness, now a snow field, now a stone block, then a window of the cottage or a pair of skis in the snow, then a sled track across the glacier edge, which vanishes out across the fjord or vanishes around the corner of an ice field, then a distant mountain peak—could it be Asinaleq or a nameless mountain further inland towards the interior?

The air above the fjord seems filled with snowflakes that whirl and scream; those are the spring-heralding terns that flap about out over the small islands; they have already begun to lay their small spherical eggs —let us collect eggs, tread carefully between the mounds and snap up that tasty morsel right away!

The snow melts, booms and distant avalanches, a cloud of snow down the side of the mountain where the avalanche can be seen; the mountain's cloak of snow frays and gains dark stripes, those are small brooks that playfully leap down the lees, down into the valleys, with the mountainside showing here and there. All the green herbs rejoice, the angelica grow thick fragrant flower clusters cloaked in green, their juicy stalks are delicious to eat with seal blubber, or without blubber, so full of a bitter sweetness, by many tastes of summer joy; but the lumpy roots are also good to chew on, a strong and sharp chew with no equal!—

The bees and the butterflies however, prefer the rosemary shrubs that scent the air with their pearly white flowers and whisper sweet things, whatever they might be. Dwarf birch with gleaming leaves, juniper bushes and blueberries sun themselves along the slopes, crowberry shrubs spread themselves everywhere the snowdrifts once lay during the spring. On the sunward sides of the river, yellow dandelions burst into bloom, while a light blue-eyed violet hides in the grass. In the pools between the sedges, a lot of small animals rustle about, the mosquito larvae hatch and the water beetles frolic.

Life defiantly breaks through everywhere, the hard winter frost having no power. The Eskimo knows from his ancestors that there is a soul behind stone and water, and no soul can die. A spirit lives in every lake and in the valley river; the mountainsides are home to spirits, the house plots and middens likewise so and the overhanging cliff edges at the fore-shore. There are old sacrificial stones on the distant mountain paths, on the long travel routes. At the foot of the Aneen mountain, out by the coast, a fossilized mountain troll stands—alas, she was once like any other human being, a woman who loved and endured her struggle in silence and secretly gave birth to her child exactly there where she, along with the child, were turned to stone, there she now stands forever more, bearing a frightful expression of pain. Boats rowing past must sacrifice blubber to her to obtain good weather for their journey; people use the ends of their fingers to put it in the distorted corners of her mouth.

The fogs come creeping in from the sea in the evening. The snow storm can, with a screech, come sweeping in from the uplands. Avalanches thunder, the rivers have voices, the mountainsides can call. Strange stone trolls poke their heads out from the cliffs, as terrifying as a bad dream. Nature is, in its loneliness, full to the brim with life and spirit; there is nothing as dead as the body whose soul has been chased away through the spiritual evil of another person, through its anger, grudge or envy. In such cases a miasma overhangs the body, and those relatives that touch the clothes of the dead and bury the body in a dolmen or in the sea, they too then walk around in a cloud of miasma until the mourning period has ended. But no soul can die, and new hunting joys, a new joy of life and new drumming songs await the souls of the dead in the tent cities of heaven or the sea. Death holds no fear for the heathen.

○

When I wintered in this place in 1905-06, the Ammassalik Greenlanders were still faithful heathens, still had angakuts[2] and witchcraft amongst them, and only very few of them had been baptized as Christians by the Danish state's missionary. (The entire tribe later swore off heathendom and let themselves be baptized). I lived with them, learned their language and customs and recorded their traditions and unwritten poems. During the summer they live in tall, light skin-tents, and during the winter they live in partially subterranean stone houses. They live in tents as separate families, but the huts are large communal houses, where as many as 10 families live together in one room, each with their place on the bench (*ittern*). From this settlement the hunters each day seek out their seals and whales, or follow the tracks of the Polar bear or fox. The sea and the fells are probably reasonably populated with game, but since the entire hunting ground is roughly the size of Zealand (2,700 sq. miles), one might understand that long distances lie between the settlements and the paths of the wildlife.

I was also minded, there, to hunt and explore, but my game was not that of the hunter. It lay in the Greenlandic settlements themselves, in the huts and in the tents, it was the Inuit drumming songs and old tales, their ivniutit and ilerqorsoot, the strange birds of the drum-singer, the liberating "spirit gust" of the poems, the small wily creatures of the magic prayer, the peculiar cave and sea animals of the legends; who in the great outside world had before heeded these treasures?[3] I took my prey home and saved it in my archive for now, to take it out, piece by piece, for closer examination and treatment. The rhythmically stylized translations that I here present, should ideally resemble the living originals. I certainly believe that I have carried across some of the soul of the natural language into my Danish texts. Some grasp of the shape and rhythm of the poems in their original language can be obtained from the Greenlandic texts which are to be found listed at certain numbers (see *33* and *53*).

None of the poems exist in the previously recorded folklore from Greenland. Only few of them are known from the West coast in variants that deviate to a greater or lesser extent, which demonstrates the great age of these poems; they belong to the common Greenlandic national poetry (for example, *11, 24* and *25*).

Overall, only a small number of poems and folk songs have been recorded in Greenland for this collection. Dr. H. Rink organized a large collection of legends and tales along the entire west coast during the last century, and in doing so also succeeded in harvesting a few drum contest songs from the southern part of east Greenland, which were published in the appendix of his considerable prose collections.[4] There are some later contributions of this type in the books of G. Holm and Knud Rasmussen; interesting, but scattered contributions. My selection here should, as a small anthology, display samples of all types of the Greenlandic arts of poetry, and thus provide the first overall picture old Greenlandic folk poetry, untouched by the European influence.

○

Will anyone listen to these new rhythms, which ring down to us from a high-northern distant culture, speaking with the voice of ancestors? Half foreign and half confidentially they call to us, because they in many aspects remind us of our own distant past, but still was born in the heart of a foreign race—this east Greenlandic people, who until recently lived secluded and forgotten, happily shut off behind the drifting ice, well preserved from the waves of Europe.

Listen to this new language from the furthest sea, sometimes a bit hard to understand, but yet so easy to hear out, happy and playful, sad and despairing voices, deep and wild sounds like bird cries, always filled with the inner wealth of its own self-existence, sated by its own wild beauty.

Rare notes are hidden in this language, ones that are only now becoming discernible. Give them a try, all you that seek and search for the harmonies of a new age! It is thoughts from the arctic night, it is tones of a winter dream from the childhood of mankind, or from its first youth. Know this youth's heathen piety and its pious politeness, its conflict, its desires and joy of life beneath the majesty of the glacier.

William Thalbitzer

Kayak Songs and Fell Songs

1. The Kayak Song of the Sea

There are always long choruses in the songs, between each verse line, consisting of aja (word with no meaning) and a directional word. I have generally omitted these choruses, which are repeated between each verse or between each line. It is, for example, stated here after the first and last verse.

Out here in the free air
I take my pleasure and joy.
        anwnaaja ajaaha ajeeh

Out here on the open sea
I take my pleasure and joy.

If the weather is really good
I take my pleasure and joy.

If the sky clears up nicely
I take my pleasure and joy.

Long may the weather hold
to the benefit of my hunt and catch!

Yes, long may it hold
to the benefit of my drum contest!
Yes, long may it hold
to the benefit of my drum song!

Out here in the free air
I take my pleasure and joy.
        anwnaaja ajaaha ajeeh

2. **Bad Hunting Weather**

With no luck in the hunt, the kayaker returns home,
and on his way he sings of the gathering clouds.

I settled my poem
on the threshold of my tongue

it was properly arranged.
But my hunt—was a failure.

Storm clouds rose from out on the sea,
the northern sky's wind-chilled drizzle and sleet,

I saw great fog banks drawing up.
They rose and pulled themselves hastily
along the mountainsides—
The wind-chilled sleet clouds
of the northern skies.

3. Kayak Signal for Catching a Bear

While the kayaker approaches the coast, he sings about his prey; the notes of his song directed at the nature of his prey, so that those listening within the settlement might know what he is bringing home.

ääjaa jaajaa jaijää aajaa hrääjai

I sing as best I can
I sing of the days catch

Now that the coast approaches
I long to sing about my catch in my poem,
of the meeting up north

we two that met
who chased each other northwards
pursuing from all sides
chased each other there

I sang my lullaby to him
and pacified him, the teddy,
until he went to sleep

I sing as best I can—
I sang my song of endearment to him—
I fetched a bear up there.

4. **Song of a Gaunt Seal**

The singer is an old hunter, who is reminiscing of the strength of his youth and luck in hunting, while he now is weakened and lives in need.

It used to be my desire to come home
with big bearded seals, often with a double catch,
yes, even with a third (I had strength then!),
a large and lovely spotted seal in addition.

Now, I always have bad luck—finally, it fails me!

The once large, fat animal that met me
out here on the waves for hunting and slaughter,
has become a gaunt spring animal.

There is now a constant state of poverty
a state of constant need and wretchedness.

5. The Kayaker Sings About His Wife

Far off the ice, people on shore see the kayaks approach.
Singing can be heard in the distance.

Now listen to me sing my chorus—*qalanaja!*
Now listen to me work out the tone—
      my drumming song, *qalanaja!*

First I must report my catch: an almost fully
      grown harbor seal,
which popped out of the water while I rowed
      towards shore.

For her sake, for she that I must protect,
for she that I always feel sympathy for.
For she is one that usually carries her burden
      on her back,
who usually moves about quietly with child
      on her back.

How go things for you so far away?
Do you also know sympathy?
Do you also have a burden-carrier,
a mother with her child on her back?

6. The Kayaker Tows His Catch Home

See him come creeping home—
        What is that you are towing, hello?
I tow a Hooded seal—a Hooded seal!
        Who is to have a shirt of the skin? Who?

Oh, it is my wife's fur that I tow!
For my wife only wears the skin of young
        Hooded seals,
she holds the common seal in contempt.

7. The Kayak on the Way Home

Hey, look, a kayak, down there, a kayak!

He carries his cargo on the rear deck,
a hunk of meat from the winter stores,
a shank he has collected from the cave in the fell.

Your wife is still angry!—

Then the kayak overturned!
He capsizes, and quickly rights himself again,
before the breakers managed to catch him—

There was a storm in the air.

8. **The Kayakers Abandoned Wife**

A person's shout from the cliff to a kayaker rowing past.
The words have to be repeated again and again due to
the distance.

Hello down there, listen, you down there,
listen kayak, kayak, kayak!
Where, where, where is your wife?

I have left her, have left her—
Where, where, where?
In the umiak, in the umiak!
Why, why, why?
Because she was almost dying from the cold
and had finally become pregnant.

She wore a shirt of the skin of
                a Hooded seal pup.
She got a small piece of blubber—

Let it drift away,
away with the current
far away into the distance!

9. **The Kayaker and the Raven**

Now hurry, speed up!
All at once, put all your strength into it!
The black beast up there,
the shy beast out there
has torn a mighty gash
in my good little kayak—
See the gash in the kayak skin here!
And then—how very like it!—
immediately grew shy and eager
and went into hiding,

as usual flew into hiding,
that beast, so black and eager.
After it! Speed up!

10. **The Strangers Kayak**

*From the cliffs at the shore a man sees an unknown
kayak approach from out at sea.*

Who is that! A man from another coast?
      An enemy?
Now it again looks as if he wants to set ashore—
Who is that down there, in the big kayak,
      that is setting in?

Now he sails this way, a stranger,
      an unknown guest,
a man from another settlement,
      a stranger among us.

How strange! I am anxious,
      the sight confuses me.

Yes, see. He is coming here!
The strange man down there—
it seems to me as if he—
as if he is suspicious of me.
Perhaps he has sung in a far away place.
Is he a drum-singer?
Perhaps he has been to a drumming contest—
      but who, who is his opponent?
How many, I wonder, has he had?
Will he also gain me as an enemy?

II. **The Foreign Umiak**

*There are legends that say that people once saw a
foreign umiak from the flooded beach at Ortunuviaq
in the Sermilik fjord. It was one of the big boat types
that belonged to the troll people from inland, a super-
natural and unapproachable skin boat. Its rowers rowed
past in silence, and they have no top hair, and if they
approach the residences of humans, or humans approach
them, they turn their faces away, so that one always sees
them half from behind. A man steers the boat—the end
of the song most likely means that Oonajuk's father
has thrown enchanted blubber into the water and thus
prevents the boat from landing, indeed on the contrary,
it drives it away.*

The foreign umiak rowers
approached from the high fell,
from the great sunny side,
with stiff necks
those rowing girls back the oars
and turn their faces away—
the closest seem to be speeding off.

What is that floating in the water,
which drives them away so quickly?
A little lump of blubber,
that Oonajuk's father threw out ....
It drives them helplessly outwards—
let them drift away!

12. **Songs While Picking Berries on the Fell**

They go to the fells to collect berries; women, girls, boys, grown and half grown—only the male hunters are absent. The blueberry and crowberry bushes lie in large round patches on top of a thin layer of topsoil across the cliffs, in mounds or in small strands along a small crack in the rock or on the lopsided step of an incline, or simply a single tuft standing between the stones. The flock spreads from cleft to cleft to gather up bags full for overindulgence at home and for winter conserving. They gather berries for hours, and when they get tired, or to show each other where they have reached, they yodel these small, drawn out ditties with the sweet tones and infinite choruses, interchanging and answering each other like the birds in the Danish forests.

In the first poem to follow here, the berry picker hears the distant song of an unknown voice, most probably a young man or woman from the neighboring settlement offering invitation to a drumming dance.

A. ALEQAAJIK'S FELL SONG

From up there—
        aja ija ijah jah—
when I climbed up to enjoy myself
picking berries on the back of the fell—
        aja ija ijah jah—
At long last in the distance
I heard a sound—far away,
a voice as from a big mouth—
        aja ija ijah jah—
deep and hollow it was heard:
will you not come to us soon?
        aja ija ijah jah—
will you ever come!
Come and have a drumming dance here!
        aja ija ijah jah—
But why do you not ever come to us,
to drum dance?

B. ITTIMANEEJUK'S FELL SONG

So deep a sorrow came over me,
settles itself heavily over my mind,
while I pick berries on the fell.

So deep a sorrow comes over me.
My sun rises quickly over it—
the sorrow settles itself heavily over my mind.

While the sea,
just off our settlement,
lies quiet in its rest.
The dear big kayakers
are in the process of travelling out onto it.

The sorrow settled itself heavily over my mind,
as I picked berries on the fell.

Lullabies
and Songs
of Endearment

13. The Little Aunt in the Amaut

*A mother sings this song of endearment to her little girl
"up there," i.e. up on her back, in the amaut (anorak
hood). The head of the little one only just peeps out
over the rim of the hood. The mother rocks her by rock-
ing her own hips, stands with closed eyes and her hands
together across her waist, crooning with a quiet voice,
more chanting than singing, the simple words to her last
born, who is named after her own deceased sister—and
thus really is her sister, as the latter's soul follows the
name into the youngest relation that is named after the
deceased.*

See her up there, a small innocent temptress!
No man has touched her,
no man has yet left his mark.
Who is she? Not the mother of my child,
not my child's sister and not its brother—
but my mother's sister!

Auntie was old, crook-backed, stuttering,
restless and fidgety, couldn't stay still,
got up early to outwit the menfolk,
that little creature also lured the males—

See how she teases,
hear how she whines,
    eja
how she can run!

14. **A Wallowing Ice Floe**

The mother compares the child rocking on her back to a small ice floe in the water that wallows up and down in the waves. Along with the traditional speech-melody, these poems often include assonances in the words and chorus-like exclamations.

How it wallows in the water!
How round and chubby it is!
How it wallows,
how round it is!
How it claps—
     ah-ja jeeq
Look up at me,
Ciamaatsiaq!

15. The Moss from the Ruined House

*The child's mother hums this little rhyming song in
a chanting tone in order to lull her little youngest to
rest. There are three subjects, with no internal connec-
tion: the wind carried a wad of moss towards her from
the old ruined house, when she was outside behind the
house wall to relieve herself. From this "toilet moss"
she jumps to talking about the big piece of cooking
stone they now have in the house, and how one of the
men wants to make a blubber-lamp or pot. The child
may be restless and want a breast: you must listen
to the voices outside the hut! And affectionately she
pinches her child between her legs.*

My drying moss approaches by a gust
from the old ruined house beyond—
Is it tucked in, my breast?

The cooking stone, the cooking stone,
how dear it was!
Is it not as good as a Harbor seal?

Oh yes—the milk in there—*aja ja!*
Were is it they are shouting from?
Over from Ipeetaleq—
How, how, what is that?

She pinched him in the crotch,
he threw himself onto the floor,
the little klutz!

16. **The Flaps of My Fur Shirt**

*The two first lines are sung slowly and melancholically;
the next words are run through in a fresher rhythm, the
tones pursuing each other, with still changing figures—
this song has, to a great extent, the character of the song
rhythm, impish in form and meaningless or enigmatic
in content.*

*The flaps in question are the lowest pointed flaps of the
fur shirt, one at the front and one behind. Those of the
woman are slightly longer than those of the man.*

My poor flaps—
how she hacks at them!
My poor flaps—
on the sharp edge of the benches.
My poor flaps—
which I have chewed tender.
My poor flaps—
which I had first chewed tender,
        jaa jaa hraa ja!

There she let them fall
on the floor with the lice!
Lice and scabies!

17. **The Children's Playhouses on the Fell**

A favorite game is to "build a house" or "tent." This consists of the children collecting some small stones of roughly the same size and color and ordering them into squares or circles on the ground, as drawings of houses and tents. The spaces between the stones represent the windows and entryways. The mother, singing, speaks to her little child:

See the sweet little windows up there
and the small stone blocks
and the poor little tents—
there is the window bench.

I go out one way,
I go in the other—
back and forth, add and subtract.

You naughty little,
you dear little—
yes, yes, oh yes!

18. **At the Beginning of Winter**

*The beginning of the song refers to the newly fallen
snow, "now the winter starts," and thus also life in the
hut, with all its captive air. The children get itchy skin.
"It is then my poor thing once more contracts scabies."*

Larger than expected,
pebbles that are much too big.
Here, here
what is this here?

Oh, this winter,
when one suffers from scabies and itches,
the horrible scabies on the fingers,
which constantly must be covered with blubber,
and bound with bands and bindings,
        aja—aja—
blubber grease!

You naughty little fellow,
who isn't nice at all,
who isn't at all pretty—
Squint is your name.

19. Fog Above, Sunlight Below

*The fog wraps itself like a blue woolen cap around the
top of the fell, while the sun still shines warmly at its
foot.*

See the fog up around the peak,
see the sunshine down around the foot!
The top of Apertilukkaak,
the whale-fell, hidden behind a curtain.
Over its steep peak,
over its mighty ridge's
rising crest
fog lies—

      awaaja!
A real fur hat!

Descend safely,
climb up safely,
lay yourself down with me!

20. **Song of Endearment and Mother's Joy over the Sex of the Child (I)**

Just as in no. 14, a mother praises her little girl, the little innocent, whom no man has touched—but who will hopefully some day mature and become tempting for men. She caresses the child's genitals while singing about them. In another, corresponding song of endearment, which we have omitted, it expressly says: Let me stroke the child over the groin! Stroke over it!— A similar magical importance is, without a doubt, attributed to these songs as to magical incantations.

The sweet, small, naughty umiak girls
have landed at Marnilik
to spread out capelins to dry!
The fur anorak, that I have sewn,
starts becoming frayed and worn,
it is moulting, it is moulting—
for Appaliartek *(the sun)*
has crumbled the skin...

They are collecting, they are collecting
crowberry heather
for the bench and the wall and the ceiling—
if only they were finished soon!

Your little crotch
is not pressed tight,
is not folded together.
Must auntie's big sister's child,
who knows how to sew,
there, there, see how easy with the fingers,
lay with you on the bench,
lay with her grandchildren?

How chubby your sweet little mound is,
how beautifully it arches,
how high it curves!
No peg has opened it,
it is sealed tight.
Are you Saartikak,
are you she who seldom smiles?

21. Songs of Endearment and Mother's Joy over the Sex of the Child (II)

The child, or its soul, is considered to be identical to that of the deceased after which the child is named, although with no regard to the gender. The same names are given to men as to women, just as men or women are more or less similarly dressed.

The little Qaanak was named after her aunt's husband, and—now that's funny—has she also not inherited an unfortunate trait from her namesake, who suffered from scabies. When she has an itch that makes the skin red, then of course it is a result of being identified with him.

Is she not little Qaanak?
He became the reason for her opening,
he became the reason for her rocking—
tightly closed,
easily rocked—
       aja—ajaja!

How strongly she smells!
Let her scratch herself so the skin reddens,
as if pierced by the nail—
how strongly she smells!

"My auntie's husband—hehehe!
My auntie's husband—hahaha!
Who suffered from scabies—hoohoohoo!
Oh how I suffer from scabies, from scabies,
the ugly, terrible scabies!"

Tightly closed,
lightly rocked—
        ajaja!

I rock and trill,
it itches and tickles—
        hrääje!

He was my auntie's, my auntie's—
Her arm, how it swings!
How it swings and sways,
her arm, her wrist and snout
(What did she do to me?)
the dear little one—my dear little one,
who is crooked and curved.

22. **A Fathers Song of his Daughter**

*When the parents had lost a newborn son, the husband
wanted to beget another son by giving the next child
the same name as the deceased one had been given.
The mother became pregnant and gave birth to a new
Kippakee—unfortunately not a boy, but a girl. (No
distinction is made between male and female names.)*

That one is still just my big little son,
that one is still just my smaller "older brother."

He was the one I wanted to try and change,
        as they say,
but I messed up my work, I did.

I will sharpen my drill right away!

That one is still just my little "older brother,"
as they say, that I will try to change,
but I only half completed the job, I did.

I will once again sharpen my drill right away.
Someone needs to be cut around
        a bit in their "bag."
For I have done a bad job, I have.

23. The Child on Mother's Arm

All Inuit children are born with a blue pigment dot on the skin, which is usually located at the bottom of the back, just above the lower back. This racial mark is one they share with the Japanese and several other East-Asian peoples.

Little whimpering dear,
little suckling dear,
cuddle up to mother!
How she burns, how she burns,
her crotch makes me warm
on my arm and hands!

Down there is the blackish-blue spot,
which will never come off
no matter how much I lick
her tiny little loins,
how shy her whimpers,
how she begs,
little bothersome girl!

Epic-Lyric
Poems

24. The Raven and the Geese

The raven had teased the geese, who now pondered how they were to avenge themselves. As they were migrating south, out across the sea, the raven asked if it could come along. It placed itself above the flock, while the others put their heads together and whispered to one another: "When we glide down to land on the water, we will quickly part ways." Some way away from shore, they began to descend, and then the raven shouted, as they parted ways: "Oh help the poor raven!" While the others settled on the water to rest, the raven flapped his wings. "You should rest too!" they said to it. "Caw caw caw, yes, since I am tired I will also sit on the water." It sat itself, but of course immediately began to sink. – Somewhat later they headed off again, with the raven once more above the flock, onwards, onwards south. They were now seriously migrating and no longer descended. The raven was anxious: "Gather closer together!" It said. The others below it whispered: "If he throws up over us, we'll fly away from him." Soon after, the raven threw up, and they flew away from him.

     The raven fell in the sea and screamed:

Ahoy, help me up!
     It's reaching my ankles now.
Ahoy, help me up!
     It's reaching my knees now.
Ahoy, help me up!
     It's reaching my waist now.

Ahoy, help me up!
     It's reaching my navel now.
Ahoy, help me up!
     It's reaching my breasts now.
Ahoy, help me up!
     It's reaching my arm pits now.
Ahoy, help me up!
     It's reaching my shoulders now.
Ahoy, help me up!
     It's reaching my chin now.
Ahoy, help me up!
     It's reaching my mouth now.
Ahoy, help me up!
     It's reaching my nose now.
Ahoy, help me up!
     It's reaching my eyes.
     A oγ–oγ

Then the water closed over it and the geese flew on southwards.

25. **Conflict Between a Wheatear and a Raven**

This little bird fable is one of the most cherished and widespread of the tales regarding the lives of animals.

The brave little wheatear comes quickly out of its nest, wailing over the loss of its husband. The raven steps up and recommends itself, but she mockingly rejects him. At which point the raven begins to use coarse language and ridicules her husband.

The Wheatear (screaming): *Ijah! Ijah!*

I have lost my husband, the great hunter, who always brought back prey. The human took him in their snares—*ijah!*

Who am I now to have as a husband? A high-browed one with big bristles, with thick loin hair, hair and beard everywhere!

The Raven: Caw caw caw!

Take me as a husband, I have a high brow, I do! And I have beard and bristles, thick loin hairs, beard everywhere!

The Wheatear (sassy): *Ijah-i!*

I will not take such a beastly lad for a husband, so horrible a brow, loathsome beard, big hideous loin hair—*ijah!* (she bursts into tears)

The Raven: Caw caw caw caw!

Why do you bother mourning your dead husband—that maggot-eater and worm-uprooter!

26. **In the Transparent Water**

The children sing about what they can see under the
thin ice on the sea bed close to shore.

See the brown trout!
With its belly full of roe,
with its big dorsal fin—
            roe-fat belly, big dorsal fin.
Now where is my little harpoon?—
            it's gone—what a shame!
And big sculpin-fry
and mighty blue mussels.

Look, there's a clam!
Its genitals are poking out,
just look at its lips—
are they turned outwards,
are they greatly swollen?

27. Your Mother's Words

The conversation of a young girl with her younger brother.

Think of the time when my
younger brother and I
were walking home from our trip on the fell,
and no people were nearby:
You must go down alone,
and fetch our cutting board!

No, I won't go down,
won't fetch it up.

Why, have you forgotten
your mother's words?
Flying out, bubbling,
like splashing water
in a deep hole, between stones
now well up:
In the little cutting board
I hid my dear amulet.

28. **Unwelcome Visit**

When the young men
come to visit,
the sisters become uneasy
but their elder brother
is, with loud shouts, called out of the house.
His forehead glistens with sweat.
Now, if possible, it is all about
       thrashing them.
Toppling them.

29. **My Extra Wife**

When Maitaq some day takes himself a wife,
then I will most definitely
            get an extra wife as well—
the big and wonderful Øse
with the wonderful big mouth.
At the mere thought, my lips
immediately take on the shape of a straw.

30. **My Vanished Delights**

How lovely they were
my vanished delights,
my dried meat supplies!

My dried meat supplies,
my delicious blood sausages,
stuffed with whale rind—
the vanished delights,
you had sold me
for my blubber bags
for my crowberries
and—yes!—for my spinning top
in the little bag.

How lovely they were.

31. **Swimming to Escape**

*A short and sad episode, the specific circumstances of
which we do not know, about a woman, "our sister-in-
law," who in anger or despair throws herself into the
water and swims across to the "island," perhaps
home to her kin.*

Our sister-in-law, ours,
sets off across the sound
towards the island.
Why are you swimming?
Because you were,
while on solid land,
standing there laughing, laughing—

She is distraught,
distraught, distraught!

32. **The Shooting Star**

You, star up there
that shines from the sky!

Your hand up there
did not hold on tight enough,
the hugging fingers let go.

So you slipped down,
but did not crash,
did not reach land.

Our earth, you did not reach.

33. **Sorrowful Lover's Ballad from the Cape Farewell Region**

The content of the lament of a young man, as his parents have refused to permit him to marry the young girl he desires. In Greenlandic "ukuarhluarisaa," the daughter-in-law his parents rejected.

I found this song to be commonly known among people north and south of Nanortalik, in the fjords closest to Cape Farewell, where the "Moravian brothers" (the Herrnhuts) for the first two centuries after colonization had education and missionary work well in hand. The Moravian's south German, mild shepherding style rings quietly through the simple words of the song, with the touching simplistic tune. Both are penetrated by the woe and agony of longing, a world-fleeing joy. The Greenlanders have legends from ancient times about embittered or disappointed people, so-called qivitoks, who chose to break away from society. The whisper of their flight to the loneliness of the fell, to hermits' lives in caves or clefts, in uninhabited fjords, far from the settlements.

The song is interesting as being a spontaneous outbreak of newer Greenlandic poetry, which seems to build upon the old way of singing with the unforced rhythm of the text and with aja-choruses, that are repeated after each line of the song. The tune, as simple as it is with its four tones, reveals that the song is not truly Inuit, but it might be one of the oldest products of the modern renaissance in Greenland, potentially linked to a real event. The author is unknown.

GREENLANDIC TEXT*

aj'a–ja' aj'a–ja'—
ukuarhliwarisa' kusanan'uarune
ukuarhluarisa' qilerteqan'iwarune
ukuarhliwarisa' sanato'nuarune
ukuarhluarisa' ilerqorin'iwarine.
Täs'an'a a'ʷhlarpona kamas'awihl'ona
kinorna sina' takujumajun'a'rrhlugo
kanerhlus'uaq ujak'ariähl'ariga
umiät uko pulán'iunuko´.
Täs'an'a ornilerpak'a as'ak'a
kak''ak'a'rtortitarhlugit
takoriáhl'arik'a ihl'u'k'a pinasut ilagim'iga'nuko
suliukak'ua kamik'a kapis'imasut torqortarim'iga't

täs'an'a a'ʷhl'arpona kamas'awihl'ona
kinorna sina' takujumajun'a'erhlugo
ja'a–ja' aj'a–ja'—.

*as written in older orthography.

Aja-jah, aja-jah
How cute she is, his rejected bride!
How prettily she wore her topknot,
      his denied bride!
How good she is at sowing, his denied bride!
How sweet in her nature, his denied bride!
I travelled from there with a turbulent mind
      never more to see her coast again.
Then I went up on the fell
      to scout into Great Fjord,
just then an umiak with women came rowing in.
Was I now to ask them to land
      there and set up tents?
Oh no, how fortunate they were to set
      up tents there!
Moving slightly closer, I shrieked out a whistle
      through my hands,
closer still I gave a fox's call.
Now I could clearly make out my three siblings,
it was they that used to rub and sew
      my boots and socks.

I travelled from there with a turbulent mind,
never, never more to see her coast again.
      Aja-jah, aja-jah!

Drum Contest
Songs

34. **Reception Song**

*An attacker approaches the land where his opponent
lives, he arrives in a big procession of umiaks and
kayaks.*

*On the cliffs stands the small flock from the settlement,
watching them approach. The attacked man's wife has
awaited the enemy—he is their guest, come to visit,
and people look forward to his arrival as one might
a play. Thrilled, she starts singing a drumming dance
on the spot where she stands. In a preaching song, she
warns her husband, as she sings of the approach of
the opponent.*

Now he comes! There they are! I wonder if
        they'll land down there!
They are from the inner fjord,
        from out west,
approaching at full speed.

Where will they land? What do they want?
What news do they bring?

There they are!
        I suppose they'll land down there?
Now he comes!
It is the ones from the inner fjord,
        the ones from out west,
who approach again at full speed,
        for drumming song,
        for drumming contest.

Hear how they yodel and sing to you!
The same small folk that you visited last year,
the ones from out west are now
              on a drumming expedition.
What do they say? How?
              I wonder if I heard that right?
They are the same small folk you visited last year,
the same dear small folk you yourself
              attacked in a drumming contest.

35. **Arrival Song**

This drumming song too is designed to be sung as a reception song, while the attacking drum-singer and his entourage approaches from out at sea.

Let me sing of the arriving singers,
who approach from out at sea!
Let me breathe of them and at them,
the swarming boats from Sanneq,
from the beach we once visited!
And let me breathe and sing against them!
Then I was almost killed
by the arrow of slander—who was it
that had spoken evilly of my soul?

What do I know? I felt horror
as my vertebrae were gripped by a stiffening.

36. Akernilik's Drum-Song Against Kunnitse

*This is a continued conflict between families, as it
was originally Kunnitse's father that had started it by
singing against Akernilik. Akernilik reminds his op-
ponent that his father had shamefully cheated him, as
he hid his drum stick in his house-box, shortly before
their singing contest, so Akernilik had to stand empty
handed when it was time to sing and drum in reply.
Now he maliciously reminds the son that the latter's
wife once, during a famine up north, had eaten of her
father-in-law's corpse.*

Your deceased father,
your deceased creator
frequently sang at me,
in spite of my never singing against him.
But this, my drum stick
had vanished from me,
it lay in his tool box
with his and your knowledge!

Still I spared him,
        your deceased father,
        your deceased creator.
But your wife ate from him,
your own Anganne
had a meal of him there—
and I wonder if you yourself weren't envious?

37. **For the Sake of a Woman**

*This is Kaaliok's drumming song of the man who had
stolen his wife away from him. When Kaaliok set
out in his umiak to pursue a drumming contest, his
countrymen shouted out to him from the beach as
he set off.*

Who will lift me?
Who will lift me to the height of the song?
When my mind is first uplifted,
progress will be possible.

They don't usually beg,
those dear little creatures that give
            birth to our children.
But she begged and enticed with words.
O heavens, that she went to him up north—
and now rumor constantly speaks
of petty angry words and squabbles—
that this rumor won't stop
            about their squabbles and fights!

He constantly beats her.

Why did he suddenly grow angry,
why was she suddenly beaten?
Oh, she is certainly innocent,
she, the wife, is surely innocent.
But he up north is envious of you,
who have lost your wife.

38. **Pitsaniarmaat is to be Punished**

The singer, a proud and self-conscious great hunter,
had been insulted by some utterances of his opponent
Pitsaniarmaat, who had, at the same time, visited the
northernmost hunting area in the otherwise uninhabited
bay of Kialineq (62° north. Lat.). He will not put up
with impertinent comments on how he treats his wife.
(The opening words regarding his anxiety about having
to attack his opponent should be interpreted as ironic.)

Oh, how worrying this is!
How worrying I feel it is to have to sing
out of my powerless soul!
How on earth did it occur to me
to direct my attack song at him!
How foolish that I must now seriously
       inconvenience myself for his sake!

When we lay up there, far to the north,
while we lived at Kialineq,
something happened, which has happened
       so many times before:
My wife made me angry, and I beat her.
I was not angry without reason,
and she was not beaten without reason,
for I was displeased with what she had sown,
my kayak cover had ripped,
       it had grown a hole.

When I went inside for a moment, people say,
that you, you scoundrel,
had made an utterance inside the house,
one quite shameless,
that I "always tend to be so damned considerate
and conduct myself so extraordinarily gently."

Oh, how stupid I was,
        that I didn't give you precisely
the same treatment—a strike,
        a jab with the knife!

A shame I acted so gently towards you,
a shame I showed so much consideration
        towards you!
You scoundrel, who carelessly provokes my anger.

39. **A Well Rehearsed Song**

In this song the attacker mocks his opponent's old
mistakes in the drumming song.

What will those wretches down south do,
should I leave now!—
See, I have left,
have come in the boat you spotted,
in the umiak, once mocked by you.
To me, your countryman,
you showed insult and mockery—
and yet you all yearned
after a short time,
yes, felt a longing for me
the day after.

So here I am, come on then!
On you go, sing against me!
As poor as I may be, after all that you say,
I am still to be your opponent.
But before I left
and all others with me,
I practiced my drumming song for a long time
and learned it by heart, carefully.
You were less lucky,
when we last met,
the two of us, for a drumming contest!
Have you forgotten how you went wrong
each moment of the song!
Pitiful, pitiful!

40. Ujaarnik's Accusation Song

*Ujaarnik from the Ittoluartivin settlement in the south
travelled up to Ammassalik to sing against Sookajik,
who seems to have wounded him deeply by
mentioning the names of his deceased relatives in his
drumming songs. The names of the dead were a taboo
for the heathens, and it was a form of sacrilege to
mention them.*

Sookajik is to have said this,
that I have lost my mind,
I am a foolish child, he says,
he views me as somewhat unintelligent—
though I am able to sing time and time again,
though I can sing drumming songs
        as often as I want,
these are my long puffs of breath.

Last summer out at sea
was full of singers,
one almost grew sick of listening to the gossip.
Oh these singers, who use the names of the dead!
I felt it like a sting to the heart,
and when I too joined the chorus,
they made me flinch with fright.
Joining in their drumming songs
I also sang about our ancestors.

41. **The Lost Hunting Bladder**

*During a kind of lament, the careful drum singer may
direct a stronger accusation towards an opponent. That
which has been lost may have been stolen by them.*

You still think I let my patience stretch too far,
        bending me before his rashness!
You think that my patience has no limits
        bending me before his provocation!
Now he is again out on a drumming contest
        expedition—
Who is it that wants to visit me on the journey?
Rumor has it, that
        my relative Qaataajuk approaches,
my proud relative approaches,
and wants to fight a mighty song fight!

Wonder what he'll use as an excuse,
what he'll cleanse himself of?
He will mention business as an excuse,
he will cleanse himself, it is said,
        with previous business—

A hunting bladder it was,
and it is mine, it concerns
my big, excellent, threefold hunting bladder,
my lost hunting bladder—

In the fjord to the west they ask:
Why must I be impeded in my hunt
just because of a hunting tool,
just because of a hunting bladder?!

42. **Killing During Derangement**

*The singer is accused of a killing; he excuses himself
through having carried it out under a fit of irresponsible
derangement, a state similar to that of an iliseetsok
(who conjures with magical means). The word "derange-
ment" should be understood with some caution, as it is
a European cultural expression, which cannot simply
be used as an equivalent.*

There he is.
        Hello, you big rumor-smith!
My angry drum-singer,
        now already slightly pacified.
He always has to turn up with his rumors!
He probably wouldn't still bring
        us rumors from Attiva
without having been slightly pacified!
How prone he is to gossip, to all things new—
        Him!

I, I will be capable of doing anything.
Very well—I committed a new killing
as these, my thoughts
had become unknown to me.
I think that it is my nature to be this way.
I think I could, unintentionally, do anything.
I act like an iliseetsok,
senseless, undisturbable,
        moving directly towards my goal.
Iliseetsut are only found other places though,
they must not come here!

Those poor iliseetsut have no
        clear understanding;
they look like the people who conjure
        far too often.

Do you have a clearer sense?

43. A Woman Denies Responsibility

I bowed my head in shame for a short moment,
I lowered my gaze to the ground for a moment,
when the singers had left.
Only then did I regain my calm,
only then did I understand this:
they thought that she had
        desired the other's spouse,
they thought that she had
        wanted to rob her husband,
my relative's husband,
my aunt's husband.

How far be it for me to steal a
        man from his wife,
how far be it from my will to ruin a marriage—
Oh no, but he had laid himself with me
        for no reason.
Woe is me, woe!

44. Two Women Engaging in a Drumming Contest

*In the first of these two songs, which reply to each other,
Marattis's mother-in-law addressed her sister-in-law
(half-brother's wife; the term in West Greenlandic is
ukuaussaq, which means 1) half-brother's wife, sister-
in-law through a half-brother or, 2) Step-son's wife,
daughter-in-law through a step-son). The older woman
(I) addresses the younger (II) in phrases that are half
ironic and hostile, half envious and conciliatory.*

I.
I still think of them,
the people from the inner fjord!
Our dear little sister–in–law
is a mischievous creature.
Yes, you have certainly made me angry
and made me your enemy!
And I, who pretended not to notice
when I went to visit them!
And look at that! You punished me,
you provided good food for me
—for me, who usually scrimps.
For you have owned him from the beginning.

Too bad he became your husband!
That I did not get him as husband myself.

II.
How she has changed over the years!
She has become almost like me.
She can barely sing any more,
hardly even make hate songs.

Since she has lost the ability to sing,
since she has lost the ability to compose—
I stopped making songs,
I stopped making poems.

45. **Drumming Song About an Angakok-Apprentice**

The "vengeance" in this song presumably consists of the "hiding places" of the angakok apprentice being disclosed. When an apprentice's secret education is revealed before their time is finished, he loses the capacity for further education, and must forever give up becoming an angakok.

Now I must be quick about it,
and avenge myself on him.
Now I must be quick about it
and sing strongly against him.
If he puts up with it, that's up to him.
While I wait here for his vengeance answer,
I will sing strongly against him!
He will show his anger towards me.
He will soon hurl mockery at me.
Will he kindly dole out his mockery,
kindly lavish his disdain?

Why do I consider him my opponent,
while he calmly stands there laughing?
Is it because you avoided paying the price,
that time you scorned an ally
(who, unfortunately, caved in)?
Is it because you avoided paying the price,
when you ruined your own relatives?
He was an orphan. May he be strengthened,
may he succeed and thrive and bloom!

The dear little big angakok in his infancy,
where was it that he tried to learn his art?
At Eelerqivik he trained himself,
and he always sought Eelerqivik,
the hiding place of the angakok,
          that was the place.

And where did be obtain his first initiation?
The angakok was initiated at Erqersivik.

46. **Akwko Sings About His Wife**

*This song is probably meant as a mixture of jest and
earnestness. The singer is the famous angakok Akwko,
who from his distant settlement furthest north in the
region—north of all easterlings—through the power of
his secretive pact with the aiding spirits, spread awe and
dread and hope of rescue among his poor fellow people
when the world seemed most desperate. He was richer
and had more wives than any other, and he often
had to punish them to keep them in check.*

*The beginning of the song is, as they so often are, bor-
rowed from an older drumming song, a song of relatives.*

This is my relatives song, that I now borrow,
old Attartik's drumming song.
It conjures the memory of the Orqua land—
You should have seen us waging
        drumming contests there!
When the songs loudly rang out,
when the drum thundered widely.
Is it Ittatak ("the laughter") who
        will sing against me?
Is he in the process of composing
        a new conflict song?

Of course—exactly—to compose about her,
for—he also—to sing about my dear little wife.
Yes, it is true I gave my wife a slap,
but should you also hit her?
I hit her, yes—
        and how could I have the heart to do so?

47. The Mermaid's Reflection

*This is a lighthearted drumming song, composed by
a husband to his wife. The author was called Mat-
takutaaq and was born at Ammassalik. She had the
experience, when she grew old, of seeing a qootsaleetaq,
"a smiling water spirit" (a kind of mermaid), in a lake
—that is at least what she said. The water spirit was
ugly and had a freckled face—her husband thinks
that she saw herself in the water.*

We were husband and wife, of the right type,
back when we cared about each other,
and thought only each other beautiful.
Eventually—she saw the face of a stranger
in the mirror of the lake.
She says that a picture reflected itself
in the black lake there—
I saw it with my own eyes, she says,
with many freckles and black spots.

When has something like that been seen before,
when has a mermaid been seen before?
It is an image to compare
for the one who recounts it.

48. **When Will He Be Here?**

Tormented by his loneliness, filled by the desire to experience something, a man sings of his longing for his opponent to arrive and sing against him.

Come forward!
I long to sing against you,
while I drift about aimlessly—
I long to drum and sing,
with a rising longing for my opponent.
Will you be here soon, as so often before?
Will you come, my great adversary?
Do you drift about aimlessly, do you not
      think of drumming contests any more!
Just let Sookajik come here!
How slow and uncomprehending!
Why does he delay?
      Does he think himself so important?
Does he think me incomprehensible, unsociable?
It has now been two summers in a row
without a drumming contest,
      without an attack—
am I, to him, not worthy of a drumming song?
Two summers in a row he has stayed away.
Finally. How different! Not like when we
      constantly sang against each other!
Hurry! It is not yet too late.
I have heard everything,
      you are angry in your heart,
filled by your unrest. You seek comfort.
The anger is upon you. The time has come.
Come now and avenge yourself!

49. The Song of the Helping Spirit Anaavak

*The helping spirit of the angakok sings about its yearn-
ing for summer. In the language of spirits, the earth is
called "our big little earth" ("little" in an endearing
way, roughly: "dear") and the summer is "the great
woman-time." When the snow melts from the fells, it is
referred to as them "smelling" or "kissing" each other.*

When you become free from sorrow,
        this our big dear earth,
which is tormented when we stamp on it!
When you now become free from sorrow,
        this our great woman-time!
When you now become free from sorrow,
        these big dear flakes of earth,
        these high mountain peaks,
already before they smell each
        other for the first time—
Now when you become free from sorrow!

50. The Song of the Helping Spirit Sanneen

*The helping spirits of the angakoks (east Greenlandic
Tartaq, pl. tartät; west Greenlandic tørnaq, pl. tørnät)
are believed to wander across the mountains, as they
step from one mountain peak to the next, or to fly
through the air. Sanneen has, on an errand for his
angakok, flown north to the Kanertivanivaq headland.
On his way, the spirit has gazed down at the settle-
ment, and established that people were "evil, as usual."*

I also took a tentative look at the fell
      out to the east,
I carefully made note of all visible to the east,
the hideous Kanertivanivaq—

Let them protect themselves
      out to the east,
let them mind their own business
      out to the east!

51. The Song of the Raven Spirit

*One of the helping spirits of the angakok Akvkos was
called Qaartuluk, "The Raven." The song is formulat-
ed as a conversation—or is a part of a ritual conversa-
tion—between the angakok, who one might imagine
would be sitting on the floor by the inner opening of
the entrance passage, with the drum at his side, in the
rapture of the trance, while the song of his raven spirit is
heard from the entrance passage, from the other side of
the "rattle skin," which hangs in front of the doorway.
The Raven Spirit recounts his dangerous kayak jour-
ney and his meeting with the bear and the storm. He
does not directly answer the questions of the angakok.*

The Raven:
Let me sing of this, when I quickly set out to
sea last autumn—when I quickly set out to sea
on the trip east—when I quickly set out to sea.
I went out too far, right out to the icy islands[5]
while these coasts showed themselves in line
with each other.

Angakok:
Did you follow the way north along them?

The Raven:
As I sought to go further north, I came straight
across the foul big bear, you know, which was just
in the process of eating the big Bearded seal.

Angakok:
But what is this I hear—
I wonder if you got a share too?
What do I hear—
are you also bringing some home with you?

The Raven:
At the place from which I usually go to sea,
I became aware of a roaring storm approaching.
Well, I thought this will be a fresh
            north-westerly!
I managed to lay my kayak paddle along the side
of the boat, but the bow in front of me
I lost from sight, as well as the big sun;
froth from my mouth trailed behind me.

Angakok:
And did you orient yourself by
the promontory there?

The Raven:
I bent to my oar again, it is my song,
I once more used the oar.
So is the sound of my song.

52. The Song of the Helping Spirit Manertaq

The helping spirit of the angakok Ajukutdooq sings about his (and thus the angakok's) enemy, who seeks to kill him by sending a tupilak (evil magical agent) that floats on water after him. It is now about turning the evil agent back at the foe, which can be done with the help of a magical song.

I still have it in my thoughts,
when Attavik came into sight long ago
floating towards him,
his spirit. This one!

Long ago it tried in vain to reach me,
without being able to.
I sang a little magic song at it:
Stop, before you arrive!
I drive you back, before you arrive!

53-54. Songs from Inland Residents (The Timerseets)

The Greenlandic angakuts often had a Timerseeq helping spirit. The Timerseets are one of the Green-landers' mythical people; they are believed to live in the interior (grnl. timeq "inland" + -seeq "one who fares there," pl. seet) from where they sometimes made their way out to the coast in order to catch seals; they would often steal from the catch of the Inuit. They didn't have boats, or kayaks, but it was said that they can wander out on the fog over the sea, or that they "use the fog as their kayak." When the Timerseek from the fell, who is out at sea, spots the skin boats of the Inuit, he is gripped by a strange terror.

These songs are sung by the angakuts during spirit summonings in the hut. "These are not our own songs," they say, "The Timerseets have composed them them-selves and then taught the Inuit to use them." Thus there are a lot of odd words in them, old fashioned or poetic words (taboo words) of uncommon use, anyway, insofar as it is known, there are no foreign loan words; the odd words are only rewritings or derivations of Inuit origin. They have been printed with letter-spaced type in my translation.

The following song was sung by Akvko as an opening when he was about to summon his helping spirit from the interior.

Ile'giak'a'	I scouted them out
kanerse'wimak'i	from the top of these fells,
qula'nemak'i	from these great promontories.
Ile'gla^wk'a'	I studied them carefully
kanerse'wimak'i	from the top of these fells,
qula'nemak'i	from these great promontories.
ajane'leqa'k'a	It was then a terror of them woke within me
nawian'e'leqa'k'a	and I began to find them frightening
a'kit'e, an'ikit'e	their skin boats, large and small.
toqume'wara	With dread, I feel that it is a matter of life and death.
erce'r^waman'a	I am terrified by this;
toqume'wara	I feel that it is a matter of life and death.

(Greenlandic text as written in older orthography.)

97

II.

Samoa jaa jaa

Let me breathe it, always and long!
When I walk across the great river,
over Greatriver to the other bank—
for I had no vessel,
no kayak, no skin boat—
let me breathe far and long
of the dear sea creatures I killed,
to the best of my poor ability,
first a good little Bearded seal,
secondly another of the same kind,
and last, in addition
the great Harbor seal
         which I could barely drag along,
I who usually frighten them away—
with difficulty I dragged them
         across the floor of fog.

55. The Woman Who Sang in the Sky

During his spirit-walk, an angakok reaches the tent-town of the dead in the sky. There he met a woman that he had known on earth, who had not been able to sing, but who could up there to her heart's content. So goes it for all who cannot sing on earth.

How did I gain the ability to sing?
When I rose to the sky,
to the big sky up above,
I was caught by a terrible tiredness,
        was caught by breathlessness.
But then I spotted my relatives:
Is it you that once existed?
Then at once I sang with all my heart,
terribly tired though I was,
breathless after my ascent.
I gradually breathed out the songs.

Magical
Prayers

56–60. **Against the Assaults of Disease**

*Sickness is always caused by an enemy or evil spirit
stealing a soul and hiding it somewhere. The danger of
disease lurks below, from the ground beneath the spot
on the bench. Asiartik is the name of the dangerous
spirit.*

I.

     éa—éa

From which animal is my bench-skin?
From the black guillemot
     I have my bench-skin,
from the skin of the Gammarus (Seaweed-flea)
     I have my bench-skin.
No disease will reach me.
     éa—éa

II.

     éa—éa

With whose lungs am I breathing?
With the lung of the caterpillar!
I am strong and healthy.
But with whose lung do I breathe?
With the lung of the bat!
I am strong and healthy.
Asiartik cannot crawl into me.
     éa—éa

III.
What lives within me?
What lives within me?
The great inland ice!
May it split!
What lives within me—
Let it perish!
      éa—éa

IV.
*The meaning seems to be this: the dog of the dawn-
ing (the morning star) is approaching. Place my dog's
harness upon it and send the messenger from the other
world, Asiartik, away. Drive him into the horizon in
the sled, to bring the lost soul home!*

      éa—éa
What now approaches?
The dog of the dawn approaches.
Place the harness of my dog on it,
send Asiartik away!
You have been sent off and on your way.

What now approaches.
The dog of the star approaches.
Place the harness of my dog on it,
send Asiartik away!
You have been sent off and on your way.
      éa—éa

V.

Here a spell is cast to counter the effect of dry rot (or a similar type of fungus found in the hut). The formula is used simultaneously with the mold being thrown out of the house.

> *éa—éa*

Remove it,
remove the fungus!
Exterminate it,
exterminate the fungus!
Move it, exterminate
the little hut's fungus,
the wretched hovel's fungus!

> *éa—éa*

61–62. **Curing**

I.

éa—éa

My souls, which I lost,
come home of your own accord!
Attach yourselves once more!
My souls, my souls
come back of your own accord,
creep in and attach yourselves!

éa—éa

II.

éa—éa

I make him alive,
only now does he live—
that human's heart.
I make him alive,
his legs and body.
Only now does he live,
his heart.

éa—éa

63–66. **Luck of the Hunt**

It is difficult to discern the polar bear in the white snowy desert. One must do magic to sharpen one's sight.

I.

     éa—éa
From the eyes of which animal
     do I gain my sharp sight?
From the sharp sight of the gull
     I gain my sharp sight.
     éa—éa

II.

Before departing the settlement, the hunter does magic like so:

     éa—éa
In the entrance opening of the tent
     I stand upright,
what comes to meet me?
An old Bull seal comes to meet me.

In the entrance opening of the tent
     I stand upright,
what comes to meet me?
A Harp seal comes to meet me.

In the entrance opening of the tent
     I stand upright,
what comes to meet me?
A Hooded seal comes to meet me.

In the entrance opening of the tent
     I stand upright,
what comes to meet me?
A Bearded seal comes to meet me.

In the entrance opening of the tent
     I stand upright,
what comes to meet me?
A Beluga whale crosses my path.

In the entrance opening of the tent
        I stand upright,
what comes to meet me?
A walrus crosses my path.

In the entrance opening of the tent
        I stand upright,
what comes to meet me?
A Polar bear crosses my path.
I wish it would crawl all the way up here!
        éa—éa

III.
The ice in the bay is melting away,
the seals are melting it away,
to the benefit of my catch,
to the benefit of my hunt.
        éa—éa

IV.
Where do I creep on my belly?
Over the ice I creep on my belly.
What do I stab there?
A Fjord seal is what I stab there.
I was sick, I got better.
        éa—éa

67. Lure for a Seal

éa—éa
What do I smell of.
What do I stink of?
I smell like an old Hooded seal,
I stink like an old Bearded seal.
éa—éa

68–69. Lure for a Walrus

I.

    kula—kula
I harpoon a walrus,
I pat it on its cheek.
You become peaceful and gentle.
I harpoon a walrus,
I pat you on the tusk.
You become peaceful and gentle.
    kula—kula
Your cheek is smooth,
your chin is smooth,
I smooth your tusks.
    kula—kula

II.

    éa—éa
Now I row around the bluff,
now I round the bluff,
what will it give me?
What will it give today?
A Bearded seal it gives me,
a big Hooded seal it gives me.
A bear it gives me.
    éa—éa

70. On the Building of a Boat

éa—éa
Did my boat get the right curve,
did I give the wood the proper curve?
Did my boat now get the right curve,
did the animal get its proper curve?
éa—éa

71. On the Boat's Amulet

éa—éa
It gives me speed on my journey,
it gives the vessel a swift speed.

72. On the Atlatl

Let's not botch it,
do not throw the harpoon askew!
Let's not botch it,
the fatso with the big front flippers,
do not throw the harpoon askew!

73. Against a Mortal Enemy's Insidiousness

éa—éa
I stroke him mildly over the cheeks—
you have been quite soothed!
I slap him softly on the cheek—
you have been quite soothed!
éa—éa

74. Against an Enemy's Hateful Thoughts

*He who does magic pulls the hood of his anorak
crookedly down over one shoulder and turns his face
away. As he utters the words, he thrusts, with an amulet
in his hand, backwards, in the direction of the person
at whom the spell is being cast.*

Off it was sent.
What is that which approaches?
There! Horribly breathing?
Across the crookedly drawn
anorak hood over his shoulder—
Off! You have been sent off.
   éa—éa

75. Against the Effect of Shooting Stars

éa—éa
Where do I lie in hiding?
Under the glitterstone I have hidden myself.
Where do I lie in hiding?
Under the moss I have hidden myself.
I am concealed, I am hidden.
éa—éa

76-78. **At the End of the Mourning Period**

After a death, the nearest mourn while observing the many taboo customs.

Keersagak's old mother used this formula when she, after her little daughter's death, according to taboo custom, had remained within the hut for half a year, and was now going down to the ice of the river or fjord for the first time. If had not been used for many years after that, but then she sold it to the young Kättuarajee, as he was to once again go out onto the ice after the end of his mourning period. He gave her his wife's headscarf in payment.

I.

      éa—éa

I step out onto the thin surface of the ice,
I step out onto the thin skin of the ice.
I have become poor now,
like the new earth, me,
this poor one here!

      éa—éa

II.

*This is for a woman, who is to sew for the first time
after the mourning period. The "pinching fingers" are
the thumb and index fingers.*

Whose claws do I have as pinching fingers?
Bat's claws are what I have for pinching fingers
       to help me in my housework.
Whose claws do I have as pinching fingers?
Crab claws are what I have for pinching fingers
       to help me in my housework.

III.

*The hunter's spell, when he has to, for the first time
after the mourning period, go out in his kayak to set
out across a bay or round a bluff. With the help of the
water beetle's attributes, he makes himself invisible and
unassailable.*

     éa—éa
Whose drape do I have as my drape?
The water beetle's drape is my drape,
I yearn to set off across the bay.
Whose drape do I have as my drape?
The water beetle's drape is my drape,
I yearn to round the bluff.
     éa—éa

79-82. **Corpse Miasma**

I.

One that has helped to bury the body of their child or one of their relatives develops a "fog" (corpse miasma) around their head and fingers. The angakok can see the miasma, while others just notice the stench. People guard themselves from the effect using spells.

He is infested with the corpse miasma,
my relative is infested with the corpse miasma.
He is infested with the corpse miasma,
the earth's surface lies in a corpse miasma.

II.

The first time the hunter goes hunting after the mourning period, he casts magic like this:

I am steaming with corpse miasma
only the dead up there have no corpse miasma.
I am steaming with corpse miasma,
only the dead in the sea have no corpse miasma.
I am hidden in my foggy miasma,
both at the flow and the ebb
and at the border of the ebb and flow.

III.

When the hunter goes hunting in his kayak:

>   *éa—éa*
I drift sideways before the wind,
>   who comes up to me?
The seals come up to me.

I drift sideways before the wind,
>   who comes up to me?
The Harp seal comes up to me.

I drift sideways before the wind
>   who comes up to me?
The seals come up to me.

"The Bearded seal, the Hooded seal,
>   the Beluga whale, the walrus"—

all are named in order from verse to verse
>   and come up to me.
>   *éa—éa*

83. Release at the End of the Mourning Period

When the grieving woman has sat on the bench inside the hut or tent for half a year, with her face turned away from the door and from the window, she is finally permitted to go down to the beach again and look for mussels or other food, and to carry out work outside. She casts the magic like this:

> *éa—éa*

My grandfather—that is an old word—
has now permitted me to do anything.
I begin.

My grandmother—that is an old word—
has now permitted me to do anything.
I begin.

> *éa—éa*

84. On the Amulet of a Pregnant Woman

*The married woman casts magic on the small spheri-
cal stone, which is to become an amulet to grant her a
child. A spherical stone is rarely found in the earth's
lap and is carefully hidden; she places it against her
abdomen, sewn into the short leather trousers that hang
about her hips like a belt, and which are called naatit.
Bent slightly forwards, with her hood drawn halfway
over her head, and with her eyes staring at the rock, she
mumbles this spell.*

> *éa—éa*
>
> You rare round stone from
> > the insides of the earth,
>
> might I have you as a fetus!
> You round amulet stone,
> might I soon have you as a fetus!
> Come here from the far side of the sky.
> Creep into my insides,
> have your effect,
> > become my child!
>
> You live in me as in the earth.
> > *éa—éa*

85. **Woman with Difficulties Birthing**

When a woman has trouble giving birth and is wracked with great pains, she uses this spell.

      éa—éa
Whose womb do I have as a womb?
The gull's womb is my womb.
Whose womb do I have as a womb?
The sea bird's womb is my womb.
        éa—éa

86. On Moving into the Winter House During the Harvest

Outside the house entrance a kitchen midden always piles up. Within it, the spirit of the midden sleeps, when the inhabitants have left the house and gone on their summer journey.

éa—éa
From whose midden do I rise?
From the house's midden I rise.
Asiartik wanders past, but he doesn't see me.
From where do I rise?
From the sediment of the midden I rise.
I am freed from the filth.
éa—éa

87. Inauguration of the Son's First Kayak

*The magic spell of a mother, when her son was big
enough to get his first kayak. Her husband built it, but
she carried out the joining of the gunwale's lengthwise
trusses, and while doing so mumbled this spell. She had
bought this from the old Ilinguakeeq in exchange for a
Bearded seal.*

  éa—éa
Whose pincers do I have as claws?
The earwig's pincers are my claws.
Whose pincers do I have as claws?
The dung fly's pincers are my claws.

The earwig's pincers make me unassailable,
the dung fly's pincers make me indomitable.
  éa—éa

88. The Magic Spell
of the Angakok Apprentice

When the heathen priest (angakok) teaches the young
man to rub the stone to summon his first helping spirit,
he provides him with the following spell.

   éa—éa
Where do I rub the stone?
On the Qaatalik I rub the stone.
Who is it that comes?
Who comes up to me, irresistible?
The spirit of the sea comes up, irresistible,
The spirit of the sea comes, irresistible,
   comes up to me.
   éa—éa

Footnotes

1. *The discovery was due to the famous umiak expedition of Holm and Garde in 1883-1885.*
2. *Pronounced anakkoq, plural anakkut, in such a way that "n" is a sound similar to "ng" in "tang," "lange" and the "k" is a lingering sound (as often seen in Swedish and Finnish).*
3. *The leader and interpreter for the umiak expedition brought us the first samples from this region 30 years ago, particularly a lot of legends as well as a couple of drumming songs and magical spells. The botanist C. Kruuse later publicized some samples of the latter type in the introduction to his East-Greenlandic flora ("Meddelelser om Grønland" Volume 49, 1912), just as samples of poetry types from Ammassalik have appeared over the years.*
4. *Rink "Eskimoiske Eventyr og Sagn." I-II Coll. 1861-66.*
5. *The static ice along the coast.*